BUGS DON'T HUG

Illustrated by
Stephen Stone

Heather L. Montgomery

SIX-LEGGED PARENTS AND THEIR KIDS

ⅈⅈⅈ Charlesbridge

Bugs aren't like us.

Mommy and daddy bugs don't give good-morning kisses. They don't tie shoes or untangle hair.
And bugs don't hug.

Rise and shine, my little bug!

For breakfast mommy bugs don't serve scrambled eggs and toast.

But baby crickets do get eggs to eat.

A mother short-tailed cricket lays extra, tiny eggs. Once her babies hatch, the special eggs will be her little ones' first breakfast.

Daddy bugs don't clean up dirty diapers.

But ambrosia beetle babies do get help cleaning up their poo.

A father ambrosia beetle cleans the hallway of his family's tree-tunnel home. With his hind legs he pushes his babies' poop and kicks it out the door.

Bugs don't play peekaboo.

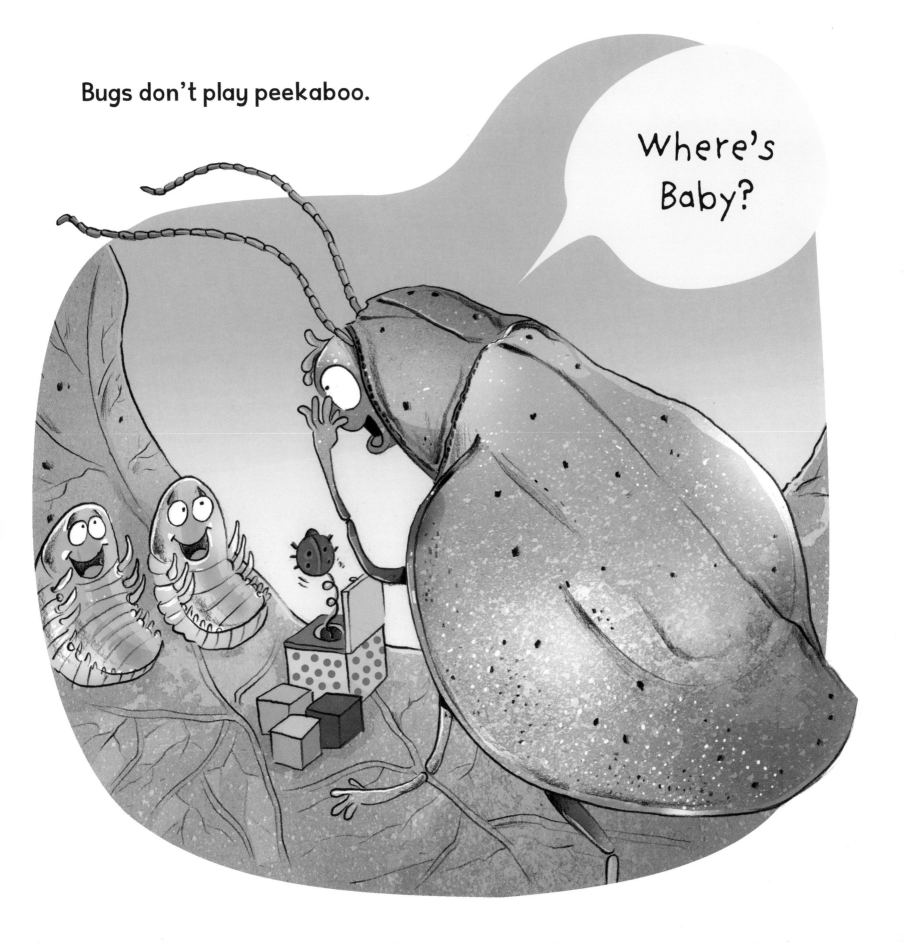

Where's Baby?

But tortoise beetle babies do get to hide.

A mother tortoise beetle hides
her young under her speckled shell.
It covers them like an armored skirt.

At lunchtime bugs don't plead with picky eaters.

But shield bug babies do demand the perfect piece of fruit.

A parental shield bug searches long and hard for her babies' favorite food. Her picky little eaters will eat only one kind of fruit, and it must be ripe.

At nap time bugs don't cradle little ones.

But baby Arctic bumblebees do snooze in snuggly spots.

A mother Arctic bumblebee presses her warm belly against her babies' bedroom. The heat she shares keeps her young cozy even in the bitter Arctic cold.

Bugs don't bake birthday cakes.

But dung beetle babies do get cake.

A mother rainbow dung beetle makes a cake of pig poop. Then she lays an egg inside it. Later, her baby eats his way out!

For dinner bugs don't make soup.

But—hang on! Burying beetles do.

A mother and father burying beetle carve a bowl-shaped hole in mouse meat. Their spit turns the meat into a soupy meal for their little ones.

Bugs don't tuck their babies in.

Night-night!

Wait!
Bess beetles *really* do.

A baby bess beetle hollows out a bed in a rotten log. Her mother and father cover her with a blanket of shavings, tucking her in tight.

A mother pill roach holds her babies on her belly. If danger draws near, she curls up to hug them close.

ARE
Bugs aren't like us.

MORE ABOUT THESE BUGS

Short-Tailed Cricket (*Anurogryllus muticus*)

Deep in her burrow a mother short-tailed cricket gently turns each egg over and over in her mouth, wiping it clean. Once her young hatch, they eat miniature eggs laid by the mother. Scientists are still trying to figure out if the eggs are a special nutritional meal—or unhatched siblings! The mother remains in the burrow, guarding the nymphs, for the rest of her life.

Central and South America
and the Pacific Islands

Yellow-Banded Ambrosia Beetle (*Monarthrum fasciatum*)

Eastern North America

Ambrosia beetles tunnel into a tree to grow a garden of ambrosia fungus. The mother beetle lays an egg in a tiny cubby, called a cradle, and fills the hole with wood chips and fungus. After hatching, the larva eats the pearly-looking fungus. When its room gets messy, the larva pushes its poop out into the main tunnel. The mother shoves the waste along to the father, who dumps it outside.

Tortoise Beetle (*Acromis sparsa*)

A mother tortoise beetle's tough shell creates a safe spot for her young to hide. When her larvae grow too large to fit under her shell, the mother climbs up and stands on top of them. If a scary wasp or ant comes by, she uses her body like a bulldozer to shove it away. Her young help out, too. They wave bits of poop in the air to scare away the predator.

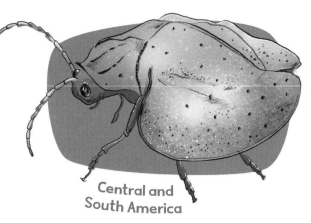

Central and
South America

Parental Shield Bug (*Parastrachia japonensis*)

A parental shield bug mother searches and searches for the perfect fruit from one type of tree (*Schoepfia jasminodora*). She then dutifully drags it home. Her journey isn't easy. The fruit can weigh three times as much as she does. Other shield bugs may try to steal it. And beastly beetles may lie in wait. If she makes it home safely, her work isn't over. To satisfy her young, she may need to gather forty more fruits.

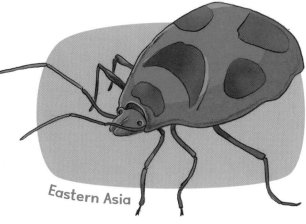

Eastern Asia

Arctic Bumblebee (*Bombus polaris*)

The Arctic

On the icy tundra a mother Arctic bumblebee wings her way to flowers. She gathers nectar (food for her) and pollen (food for her young). Back in her nest she releases heat through her abdomen. Even if the air outside drops to freezing, she can warm the brood clump (where her larvae live) to a toasty 86°F (30°C).

Rainbow Dung Beetle (*Phanaeus vindex*)

The mother and father rainbow dung beetle work for days digging a nursery and dragging dung into it. The mother makes a dung cake the size of a golf ball. To keep it moist she "frosts" it with clay. Finally she lays an egg at one end. Then she begins all over again, repeating the process up to thirty times in just one season.

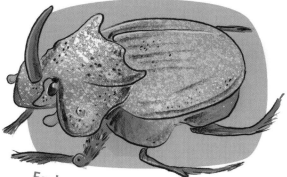

Eastern North America

Burying Beetle (*Nicrophorus vespilloides*)

When a mother and father burying beetle discover a dead mouse or bird, they strip off its fur or feathers and bury it. Underground they slather the body with a liquid from their rear ends to clean it. Then they dig a hole in the mound and add their spit to predigest the meat. The young gather at the hole for a nutritious meal. The parents will also spit food directly into the mouths of begging larvae.

North America, Europe, and Asia

Bess Beetle (*Odontotaenius disjunctus*)

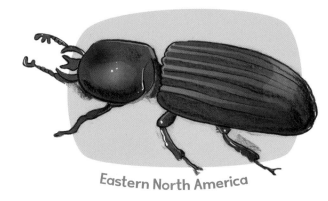

Eastern North America

A larval bess beetle's jaws are too weak to rip tough wood, so its parents prechew its food. The larva eats the wood with a side dish of poop. When it's time to pupate, the parents and young work together to make a protective covering. The adults pile on wood shavings and poop from the outside, while the young shapes the covering from the inside. If the larva's "blanket" is damaged during pupation, the parents or an older sibling patch it up.

Pill Roach (*Perisphaerus semilunatus*)

Pill roaches are mysterious creatures. No one knows how young pill bugs get their food, but scientists have a guess. In addition to carrying her young, a mother pill bug may nurse them. Near the joints in the mother's legs are several small pits. The purpose of the pits is unknown, but the strawlike mouths of the young are just the right size to fit into them. Perhaps the young stick their mouths in and suck up roach milk. Mmmm—nutritious!

Southeast Asia

MORE TO READ

Ant, Ant, Ant! (An Insect Chant)
   by April Pulley Sayre,
   illustrated by Trip Park
   (NorthWord, 2005)

The Beetle Book
   by Steve Jenkins
   (Houghton Mifflin, 2012)

Bugs Galore
   by Peter Stein,
   illustrated by Bob Staake
   (Candlewick Press, 2012)

Some Bugs
   by Angela DiTerlizzi,
   illustrated by
   Brendan Wenzel
   (Beach Lane, 2014)

AUTHOR'S NOTE

Bug Mommies and Daddies?

We don't usually think of insects tucking their kids into bed, making dinner, or cleaning up after their young. Most insects don't take care of their offspring—they lay a bunch of eggs and take off. But some insects do spend time caring for their young. And they do so in surprising ways.

Scientifically Speaking

In this book I used playful language to compare insect and human behaviors. Scientific language is different. For example, the scientific term is *insect*, not *bug*. A young insect is called a *larva* or *nymph*, not a *baby*, and it is often referred to as *it*, not *he* or *she*. In order for an insect to grow up, its body must go through the process of metamorphosis. A bess beetle larva, for example, doesn't actually go to sleep in a "bed." Instead, it becomes a pupa. From the outside the pupa looks peaceful and still, but inside amazing changes are happening. Finally the beetle emerges as an adult with wings.

A NOTE TO PARENTS

Children are fascinated by little creatures. Your reaction to that fascination will affect your child for life. What will your reaction foster? Respect? Caring? Curiosity?

   Share your child's wonder of the world. Stop to watch a line of ants. Turn over a dead log. Scoop some bugs from a pond. (And discuss why you will put them back.)

   Discover together!

In memory of my mother, Carol Sue Martin—H. L. M.

To my loving wife, Claire—S. S.

With thanks to the many scientists who shared their knowledge and passion with me.
These include Dr. George Beccaloni, Dr. James Costa, Dr. Sheena Cotter, Jacqueline Dillard,
Dr. and Mrs. Thomas Eisner, Dr. Douglas J. Emlen, Dr. Lisa Filippi, Dr. Terrence Fitzgerald,
Dr. Jennifer A. Hamel, Dr. Bernd Heinrich, Dr. Jiri Hulcr, Dr. Joella Killian, Dr. Scott Kight,
Dr. How-Jing Lee, Dr. Hiromi Mukai, Dr. Christine Nalepa, Dr. Dana Price, Dr. Michael D. Toews,
Dr. Paula A. Trillo, Dr. Jill Wicknick, and Dr. S. Hollis Woodard.—H. L. M.

Text copyright © 2018 by Heather L. Montgomery
Illustrations copyright © 2018 by Stephen Stone
All rights reserved, including the right of reproduction in whole or in part in any form.
Charlesbridge and colophon are registered trademarks of Charlesbridge Publishing, Inc.

At the time of publication, all URLs printed in this book were accurate and active.
Charlesbridge and the author are not responsible for the content or accessibility of any website.

Published by Charlesbridge
85 Main Street
Watertown, MA 02472
(617) 926-0329
www.charlesbridge.com

Library of Congress Cataloging-in-Publication Data
Names: Montgomery, Heather L., author. | Stone, Stephen, 1974– illustrator.
Title: Bugs don´t hug: six-legged parents and their kids /
  Heather L. Montgomery; illustrated by Stephen Stone.
Other titles: Bugs do not hug
Description: Watertown, MA: Charlesbridge, [2018]
Identifiers: LCCN 2017012705 (print) | LCCN 2017030636 (ebook) |
  ISBN 9781632896698 (ebook) | ISBN 9781632896704 (ebook pdf) |
  ISBN 9781580898164 (reinforced for library use)
Subjects: LCSH: Parental behavior in animals—Juvenile literature. |
  Insects—Behavior—Juvenile literature. | Insects—Infancy—Juvenile literature.
Classification: LCC QL762 (ebook) | LCC QL762 .M66 2018 (print) |
DDC 595.71563—dc23
LC record available at https://lccn.loc.gov/2017012705

Printed in China
(hc) 10 9 8 7 6 5 4 3 2 1

Illustrations created by combining expressive lines, hand-painted textures,
  and a bright, bold color palette in Photoshop
Display type set in Populaire by Ricardo Marcin & Erica Jung
Text type set in Helenita by Rodrigo Araya Salas
Color separations by Colourscan Print Co Pte Ltd, Singapore
Printed by 1010 Printing International Limited in Huizhou, Guangdong, China
Production supervision by Brian G. Walker
Designed by Sarah Richards Taylor